SPIRITUAL C
AND YOUNG ADULTS

*How to Connect with your Higher Self
in the 21st Century*

BRANDON HUSSEY

Copyright 2020 All rights reserved.

No part of this book may be reproduced in any form on by an electronic or mechanical means, including information storage and retrieval systems, without permission in writing from the author, except by a reviewer who may quote brief passages in a review.

TABLE OF CONTENTS

Preface 1

A Little About Me 2

What is Spirituality? Why would you want to be Spiritual?.. 3

Part I: The Building Blocks: Dopamine, Discipline, Mindset . 5

    Dopamine 5

    Discipline 7

    Mindset 8

Part II: Comfort 10

    Put Down Your Phone 11

    Cold Showers 13

    Day to day Energy 15

Part III: Wellbeing 17

    A Bad Situation 17

    Coming to Terms with Yourself 17

    What People Think about You 18

    Positive Affirmations 20

    Health 21

    Go Running 23

    Spend Time with Nature 24

Part IV: Meditate 26

Part V: Gratitude 29

What's there to be Grateful For?..29

Cutting Things Out..31

Part VI: Mindfulness...32

Live in the Moment...32

Balance..34

Benefits of being Mindful:...35

Part VII: YOU WILL NOT BE HAPPY 37

Dukkha..39

Self Acceptance...40

What I Learned From Other Cultures 41

What Should I do if I'm Depressed?....................................43

Part VIII: Change 45

Energies...45

Dealing with Negative Energy...46

People are Going to Hate You 47

Sex Transmutation 48

Part IX: Live Your Life...51

Contemplate 51

To Conclude 54

Acknowledgements 56

PREFACE

The first thing you'll notice about this book is that there isn't a lot of fluff. This book is going to walk you through on how to take clear, actionable changes to your life with the goal of connecting with your higher self and making your life instantly better the moment you finish each chapter.

Another reason I decided to write this is because I see spirituality fading away in the world as cheap and easy ways to exist rise and dominate our lives. The 21st century is a hard place for an adolescent to prosper in the 1st world. That sentence may sound ridiculous but I will explain why this is in the book. I also noticed that all of the other books directed towards spirituality and positivity for teens and adolescents in general are not written by adolescents. They are all written by older people in their 40s and 50s that are recalling or ascertaining what it is to be an adolescent based on their own experiences decades ago.

I draw most of the information from books I've read, and always being a fan of history and philosophy, I've read quite a few. For the most part I'm going to combine long-established philosophies such as Stoicism with Buddhist and Christian principles to show you how to achieve a state of enlightenment where you can finally be aware that most of modern life and the American Dream is false advertising, and that you don't actually need to do much to live happily and connected to your higher self.

A LITTLE ABOUT ME

Who am I? Why should you take my advice? Sure thing, my name is Brandon and I'm twenty years old. I've loved books all my life and especially love history. I'm originally from Jamaica but live in Miami, Florida. I've been through a lot of change in my life, both good and bad. I'm sure you can relate. In the book I often reference my own life experiences, from going to boarding school in Pennsylvania to playing collegiate sports and joining the military at 17. At the time of writing this, I'm enrolled at a military-based university and am pursuing a degree in Political Science, along with a minor in History and Leadership. I have a passion for helping others, always striving to see the good in others and the value that they can bring to the world. Outside of my material accomplishments, which don't really mean much, I exist in this world in a state of complete peace and acceptance for who I am. That's really what I want to share with you through my words that make up this book. I believe that every person's life is like a book, full of different chapters and experiences and positive lessons to be shared, and I hope that you can learn some from mine.

WHAT IS SPIRITUALITY? WHY WOULD YOU WANT TO BE SPIRITUAL?

The most simple definition of spirituality is the ability to connect to the human spirit as opposed to material and worldly things. That's it. However, this relatively simple concept is now extremely hard to attain because of the way that our world is designed. Gone are the days of simplicity that allowed the young adolescent to live and to learn as a human should and be guided by his or her community to become a strong and productive member of society. We are being raised by machines and the government. We are in cages now, might I add. You see, a very long time ago, the most powerful of people would simply enslave their workers and place them in cages and tell them to work. This is why humans have been able to control other humans and profit from it, because you can put a knife to a human and tell him to work for you now or else you will kill him tomorrow. You can't put a knife to a cow and tell it to produce milk or you will hurt his family tomorrow. The only difference is that now you cannot see the cage, so to the simple minded and unspiritual, you are free. Society allows us to choose what we want to work on and where we want to live, giving the illusion of freedom. What they do not tell you is that there are institutions in place to discourage activities and thoughts that make you less human and more like part of a machine. Such is the story of your enslavement.

When you eventually master the art of building spirituality (yes, it's a process, not an instant transformation), you will be quick to notice that every aspect of your life will get better. You will find comfort in times of hardship, you will persevere through discomfort, and you will learn the ability of living in the present and stop the constant observation of future and past. Personally, I believe that the most valuable skill you will learn is unlocking the spiritual energy that you have inside of you and putting it out into the world for positive productivity and leadership.

PART I: THE BUILDING BLOCKS: DOPAMINE, DISCIPLINE, MINDSET

I'm going to outline some concepts that will become common themes on your spiritual journey. Understand that you're not going to change overnight. For most people, including me, our states of mind and ultimate resolve is the result of years of conditioning. In other words, it took you years of training to become a man or woman without action. You weren't born that way. In fact, it was quite the opposite. If you can, remember the days of being a child where everything was a new experience to you, and you were excited to experience new things. You were able to look out the window and observe what was going on for the longest time and you didn't feel drawn to something else after six seconds. After years of being experienced to artificial levers that bring you false happiness, that gratitude that you felt for simply existing is now gone. Understand that it is not your fault, or anyone else's fault for that matter. Do not be resentful to your parents or to your God. Step one is recognizing that you, like every person, have it within yourself to return to your natural state of being.

Dopamine

The good old reward chemical. It never fails us, right? Wrong. It fails us every day. It's the reason our monkey brain convinces us that it's a better idea to play on our phones instead of pursuing what it is you really, truly want. Think of dopamine like a binary coding in the machine of our brains. A one means good, do more of that. A zero means no, do less of that. If you have a donkey and you sit him down and stuff him with cake, he's just going to sit there and get stuffed with cake. Sure, his enjoyment for the cake will probably go down over time, but eating the cake is going to be priority number one and will forever be more pleasurable than say, walking ten miles with a load on the donkey's back.

Understand that the modern world is full of dopamine hits that are specially crafted and engineered to get you, the product, addicted. You'll spend time and money on them and they will trick your brain into believing that they are good. Your brain doesn't care at all about achievement, that is instead the imperative of your rational (human) conscious. All your monkey (animal) brain wants is to feel 'good', and it doesn't care about how it feels good, only that it does. I will go into the things that can rob you of your spiritual potential later on but for now you must recognize that 1) you are addicted to physical things like your electronics, and 2) that you can break these addictions and free up your brain's 'will' to pursue what you really want in life, which is, again, what I think the best benefit of being spiritual is.

When I was going through basic training for the military, my monkey brain was starved of dopamine. I wasn't allowed to use my phone, eat junk/ sugary food, access the internet in any way, watch tv, use tobacco, drink alcohol, sit around all day, or basically anything else that we see as relaxing or pleasurable. What the military was trying to do was get my full attention so that when they broke down the civilian inside of me, they could train me to be what they wanted me to be, and have my full attention doing so. What I learned from this experience is that when I was in that state of not having access to anything I thought was pleasurable, I was incredibly motivated to do anything. Let me say that again, I was incredibly motivated to do anything. The clouds of addiction were cleared from my mind and for the first time since I was a child, I was able to really, clearly, think. I not only got closer to God but who with who I was.

Discipline

I think that you can train a person to be disciplined only to a certain extent. Past that point, a person can only be truly and completely disciplined if they are trained in understanding discomfort and having self control. Take people in the military for example. I know lots of people that were in the military and when they get out they stop working out and taking care of themselves because that discipline was imposed on them. To really be disciplined, you have to want to be. I found that the best way to achieve discipline is training yourself to be uncomfortable so that everything that's hard becomes easy.

Discomfort is something that our ancestors had to deal with. It was a fact of life, It wasn't optional. Having to, say, walk ten miles to and from school or work every day because there was no other way. Yeah, sucks. Now because of all this discomfort, as humans naturally do, they created and found ways to eliminate discomfort from their lives and the lives of their offspring. What we're left with is a world that does everything for us. For a lot of people, including myself, it's hard to sit down and read a book, for example. It's uncomfortable to sit and do something that I know deep down that I want to do because there are so many distractions. What discipline does is it allows you to be okay with that discomfort and find peace in your current activity. Marcus Aurelias, one of the earliest proponents of Stoicism, said "Be as a horse after a run. A dog after he has tracked game. A bee after he has made the honey, so a man when he has done a good act, does not call out for others to come and see, but he goes on to another act, as a vine goes on to produce again grapes in the season.". The point of this quote is to do what it is that is your purpose in life and do not seek validation or other alternative motives but simply let it be.

You can build your discipline by regularly performing activities that increase your tolerance for pain and discomfort (without harming yourself, of course). You will learn about these practices later on in the book.

Mindset

It's no secret that your mindset dictates most of the results you will get in life. In other words, you will reap what you sow. "As a Man Thinketh" is a great book written by an English author in the early 20th century. He claims in this book that the outcome of your life is determined by the actions that you put forth, which are beforehand determined by what you tell yourself and the thoughts that you grow inside your head. If you are a person that constantly gets caught up in the media and constantly thinks negatively, you will in turn exude that negativity into the world and the world will give that same negativity back to you. Instead, have a positive mindset and don't believe the things you tell yourself when you are sad and alone. When I got kicked out of high school I constantly held a melancholy frame and thought that the world was out to get me. It wasn't until I started thinking positively and removing myself from negative emotions and people that I started to get a return on my positive investment from the world. Everything that I possibly wanted in that moment, I now have.

Don't tell yourself that you're a king or a deity, but rather that you're a good person and you're going to achieve whatever you put your mind to. You're honest, hardworking, and honorable. Before long you will indeed see yourself acting like what it is you're telling yourself that you are. Now through these actions, you will begin to see positive progress in your life and you will attain what you want out of life.

PART II: COMFORT

People are rational and desire to be comfortable. It's why we have things like air conditioning and hot water in the shower. We can use it to motivate ourselves to do things we wouldn't otherwise do. One thing I've learned in life, especially in my late teens, is that there can be no success without a little discomfort. You're going to have to get comfortable being uncomfortable for any kind of growth, and that is especially true for spiritual growth. You don't have to be completely comfortable all the time.

Siddhartha Gutama, the founder of Buddhism, taught his followers that life is discomfort, and that it's akin to riding on an oxcart with a shaky wheel. He argued that you can, however, learn to be comfortable amid the shakiness.

My high school wrestling team was ranked top ten in the nation. We were good. Those guys were warriors. It was the norm to lose a few pounds throughout the week healthily in order to get to your weight class, wrestlers including myself were often overweight after a junk-food filled weekend. In the days leading up to my match when my stomach was empty and I was working hard every day, I realised something. I got closer to God. I'm not promoting any religions in this book, only spirituality and inner connectedness. I felt like I could communicate with God by just meditating, whereas before I needed to go to church. Not eating the junk food that connects up the dopamine receptors in my brain made me not only more motivated, but more spiritual. I'm not saying that fasting will make you more spiritual, what I'm saying is if you cut out the things that bring you artificial, short term happiness, like junk food, sugary drinks and other sweets, your brain will feel more happy and healthy, and it will reward you for it.

Many of the life changes I'll be putting forth in this book require a certain level of discomfort. The greatest spiritual shamans and religious leaders have all mastered this art. Rich and powerful businessmen have mastered this. I guarantee you that anybody who has gone and found peace in their lives has too.

Put Down Your Phone

What I want you to do as you're reading this is put down your phone. If you're not expecting an important call, turn it off. Do it right now. Do it if you are really serious about changing your life. Don't continue reading until you have done so. If you don't have the discipline and willpower to turn off your phone for a short period of time, then how will you have enough discipline to fulfill your true purpose in life?

There are many reasons why phones are not conducive to spirituality but before I get into that, I want to show the importance of meditation. Meditation is going to be a key principle from here on out so you might as well get comfortable with it. It doesn't matter what religion you are or where you come from, meditation is more than just connecting with a deity or God or multiple Gods. Meditation is one of those skills that has a wide range of successful outcomes, from productivity to happiness and spirituality.

The reason you had to turn off your phone while reading these few paragraphs is because it's the opposite of meditation. This, in a way, is your first form of breaking free. Most teens can't exist for short periods of time without contact with their phones. You see it all the time, when you go out. People are just looking down into their phones as if the real world doesn't exist. I saw a young man yesterday walking down the street just staring at his phone. He couldn't just walk to the store without looking at it. If you recall what I said earlier about dopamine, your brain sees things as either a 'one' or a 'zero'. Right now, your brain sees your phone as a 'one, if not a 'two'. Most people are afraid of existing without their phones, it makes them uncomfortable to just exist without constantly pulling the dopamine lever. Don't worry, though, because soon you're going to have the discipline to break that habit and other things in your life will bring you that natural joy and fulfillment that your brain thinks it's getting from the phone.

Okay, you got through that much without the phone. You can turn it back on now, if you want to. Just know that whoever texted or called you, can probably if not certainly have waited. I guarantee they wouldn't mind.

I'll share another Basic Training story. I remember vividly the day we graduated. It was a sunny day in late August. We had permission to go out and spend time with our friends and family, to walk around on base. It was the first time we had full access to our phones in almost three months. I remember having it in my pocket, always attached to me, like rectangular aluminum alloy appendage. It felt strange, that somehow a piece of my entire world was inside the rectangle in my pocket. I realized that my life was connected to it. I remember asking myself, why is this thing so important? I felt like breaking it.

At the siege of Troy in ancient times, the Greeks were attacking the city of Troy. They couldn't get into the city so they came up with a plan of deception. They pretended to abandon the siege, and get on their boats and sail home. They sent the Trojans inside the city a giant, wooden horse. The Trojans, in all their confidence and arrogance after just having won the battle, thought it was a farewell gift from the Greeks, a gift of peace. They opened the gates and let the wooden horse inside. Out poured some of the best soldiers that the Greeks had to offer, and they opened the gates for the Greeks who came rushing in. Troy fell and the Trojans were defeated because they let something inside that was presented as a gift.

I believe that cellphones are like a modern Trojan horse.

Cold Showers

This one's going to be a little harder than just putting down your phone. So buckle up. Even though they are difficult and uncomfortable, I would argue that cold showers have been the single most important lifestyle choice that brought me to take risks in my life and make changes. I firmly believe that they played an important part of why I decided to join the military when I was seventeen years old and then, one year later, go to college and pursue my degree.

Cold showers make everything in your life easier. It's going to make meditation feel good and it's going to make you feel gratitude like you've never felt before. You don't have to just turn your shower to the coldest setting and just jump in. Actually, if you're not used to the cold water I wouldn't recommend it. You can start by taking a warm shower and then turning it to lukewarm while you're still in there. After a couple minutes, turn it to a little colder but not Antarctica cold. The next time you take a shower, have it at a nice cool temperature and then just put your hands and feet in there until your body acclimates to it and then take a full shower like that.

You will probably notice that a couple things are different with the cold showers. Usually when you get out of a hot shower, you feel cold and want to put on clothes. Now, after your cold shower, you feel warm as you get out and feel a sense of freedom. There are lots of important things that go on while you're in there, too. Your brain produces dopamine and you feel good when you get out. They accelerate your metabolism and immune system, and your body produces anti-depression hormones. You may feel more alert and just 'in flow', as I like to call it. You just accomplished something, a real thing. You just made your body more resilient to extreme temperatures, and did something that most people can't do.

You may notice that while you were in there, you felt one thing that you haven't felt in a while. Your heart was beating fast, your chest was pumping, you were breathing hard, your eyes were wide open, and your adrenaline was running. You felt alive. You were alert and in the moment. You weren't thinking about the future and the past. That's what life is supposed to be, you're supposed to feel alive and actually living.

Since spiritual living requires you to live a disciplined life, mastering the art of the cold shower is going to be a handy instrument in your toolbox.

Day to day Energy

Energy is a huge topic so I'm going to have to break it down into bits and pieces. What you just did by going a couple minutes without the prospect of looking at your phone redirected your energy in a different direction from where it usually is. Different things in our lives take up energy throughout the day and when you start to eliminate them, you'll get your energy back and you can refocus that energy on things that you really want to do. Because you really don't want to scroll through instagram, watch snapchat stories, watch youtube videos. You don't care. Your monkey brain cares and like I said before, it doesn't give a damn where that dopamine comes from as long as it comes from somewhere. You're smarter than your monkey brain so recognize that feeling deep down that you know what is good for you and listen to it.

Every week we have a certain amount of energy, imagine it as a hundred points of energy. Every day you have a certain amount that you wake up with, think of it like the willpower for that day. Think about searching through your house for an important document at midnight after a long, hard day of work or school. Yeah, not gonna happen. Think about and really consider how much of your valuable energy that you expend each day scrolling through social media. It's not healthy, it's not productive, and you don't want to do it.

PART III: WELLBEING

A Bad Situation

We can control our reactions to the bad situations in life. This is an idea that mostly comes from the ancient Stoics and also from the Buddhist story of the second arrow. It goes like this- The Buddha asks his followers if it's a bad thing if you're just walking on a street and you get hit with an arrow. All of his followers agreed that it would be bad. He then asks them if it would be bad if they got hit with a second arrow right after. Again, they all agreed. The Buddha explains to his followers that the two arrows are metaphors for life. The first arrow is anything bad that happens to us, the second is our reaction to it. Sometimes the second one can be more harmful than the first. We can get angry and upset at a bad situation, but that second arrow is always up to us.

Coming to Terms with Yourself

People's egos are huge. When I first went to college I realized that people didn't raise their hand to answer questions. Why? Because they have an ego. They don't want to look stupid. They don't want to get out of their comfort zone.

So it's no secret that people care about what other people think. We want to be accepted by the tribe. Back in the days of the cavemen, we all needed the tribe. If we were seen as unfit or incapable, we were abandoned by the tribe and we would die. It's basic human nature to want to be accepted by conforming to what everyone else is doing. Why? Because when you step outside you risk being banished or ostracized by the tribe. And you don't have the confidence to take those risks so you just do the same thing as everyone else. Let me tell you right now that your monkey brain is failing you again.

What People Think about You

It's in human nature to want or desire to be a part of the tribe, to be accepted. It's ingrained in our biological nature because not too long ago if you were rejected by the tribe you would die. We needed each other to take down large animals and share resources for the betterment of the community. So most people have a fear of not fitting in, and they do things they wouldn't normally do and spend money on things they can't afford because that's how you fit in. It's no secret that money talks, and when you go somewhere in an expensive car for example, it's going to turn heads. It's the easiest way to get attention. And honestly, it works at doing that. For a lot of people, this stems from issues that they faced in their childhoods. It's usually related to the love and attention that you didn't get when you were a kid. My parents were married growing up but my dad was never around. My mother was a working woman and she worked hard. As a result she wasn't there with me at home too often. I, like most people, spent a good amount of my time and energy growing up trying to fit in and get attention from the tribe. It's part of what makes us whole, we need to feel like we're accepted and important.

Ask yourself, and answer honestly, what does attention from other people really do for you? If they like you, will that make you smarter, more wealthy, or better at your skillset?

What I learned from working door to door sales in Miami and going to hundreds of strangers' houses per day is that most people that drive luxury cars like Mercedes Benz and BMW can't really afford them. They never bought the hurricane impact windows and doors that I was selling because they knew their credit couldn't handle the payments and they didn't have enough cash. They would rather have a car that impresses people and turns heads than equipment that could protect their homes and loved ones in a disaster. The people that did buy them, however, always fit a specific mold. Keep in mind that impact windows and doors aren't particularly cheap, so these people were spending at least six thousand and at most seventy thousand dollars depending on the size and quantity of the windows. The people that did buy them were always responsible people. They usually drove a modest car, like Ford or Honda. They are the type of people that didn't care about what people thought about them and drove a fuel efficient car that could comfortably get them from point A to point B. If you stop caring about what people think you're going to 1) value money less, like you should and 2) become more free and reduce your stress because you're not trying to impress anyone. Impressing people takes up a lot of time, money, and energy that can be much better spent on improving your life, working on your business, and being healthy and ecstatic about life because your happiness doesn't depend on other people.

Is it going to be hard to cut people out of your life? Yes. In fact, it's going to be extremely hard. Realize that a lot of the people in your life don't actually add any value to your life. Keep the people close that do add value to your life and keep them close. You'll realize that these are the people that will return the positive energy that you bring to them and you'll benefit from their energy too. Encourage them and motivate them when they're down and it will enrich your own life by putting that good energy out into the world.

Positive Affirmations

Positive affirmations are widely used to bring out the greatest potential in people and bring up their confidence through repetitive 'affirmations', or basically, repetition of positive mantras to one's self. This can work for motivation, self-confidence, connecting with God, and much more.

The reason why it works is because your subconscious brain exists. Your subconscious takes information that it's fed on a day to day basis, and internalizes it. The bad part is that even though it can be used to better yourself, it's a double edged sword. If people around you are telling you that you're going to fail or what you're doing is pointless, your subconscious will internalize that too. The worst part is if you're telling yourself things relating to being a failure or a loser, you might forget about it in a couple hours but your subconscious won't.

Tell yourself constantly that you want to get closer to your higher self. Always tell yourself that you're a good person, and that you bring positivity into the world and people around you. Do this throughout the day whenever you can, and especially right before bed. Before you know it, you'll automatically start acting like it without knowing because your subconscious is absorbing this information and like James Allen said in his book *As a Man Thinketh*, your positive thoughts will lead to positive action, which will in turn lead to positive results.

Health

Health is one of the most important parts of connecting with your spiritual side. Understand that your own body is a temple. It's the temple in which your soul resides, you need to take care of it. In fact, you have an obligation to take care of it, if not for yourself then for other people in your life. You need to be healthy so that you can be able to bond with your children and your grandchildren and continue to be alive.

When I was young and my father was still a professional athlete, he did not appreciate his athletic gifts. He was always an athlete, and was doing his sport professionally since he was 13. For decades, because of his athletic gifts, he got away with not taking care of his body. He drank often, went out late, and didn't sleep much. The problem was that he didn't begin to feel it until he got older and realized that he wasn't invincible. He would always tell me that when you're young you feel invincible and then you get older and you come down to Earth when you start hurting. All those years of an extremely active but also unhealthy lifestyle took a toll on him and a couple years ago he decided to change so that he wouldn't die younger than he should. What I noticed was amazing. When he fixed his diet, quit drinking alcohol, and stopped going out and started sleeping at night, every single other area of his life improved. Since then, our relationship has become much closer and stronger. We encourage each other to avoid unhealthy practices and eat healthy, avoiding sugar, salt, and other junk food. He tells me that he's closer to God nowadays and because of his diet, he can see things much more clear. He tells me he has much more energy on a day to day basis. He's happy.

My father became healthier and now he's much more happy and at peace with himself and God. Although it has so many benefits, it's hard to become healthy in the modern world. It takes discipline every single day to stay healthy. It costs time, money, and energy, but in the long run it'll pay dividends because of your low doctor fees and your abundance of energy that you have to put into your family and business.

Your diet is one of the most important parts of living a spiritually connected life. Your body is a temple, and like a well-oiled machine, your brain will work more efficiently and you'll feel the energy more smoothly if you're on top of your diet. I never learned anything like this growing up, I had to learn by researching online when I had to lose weight to wrestle in high school. What you want is easy to digest food so that your body's inflammation levels can reduce.

Here's my diet back when I used to cut weight for wrestling. I ate turkey or chicken meat, lots of fruit and vegetables, walnuts or coconut oil for fat calories. No juice or any other liquid but water. This diet is great because these foods pass quickly through your system so that you're not spending too much time and blood digesting food. The fog inside of your mind will clear up and you'll think much faster and become stronger. This diet is particularly designed for losing weight and maintaining a very low body fat.

I don't have to lose weight anymore, but I still maintain a healthy lean body at 8% body fat with this diet right here. It's chicken and turkey meat, lots of fruits and vegetables (apples, bananas, tomatoes, carrots, lettuce, green beans), oatmeal (traditional), sweet potatoes, whole grain bread for the sandwiches, walnuts or almonds, and eggs. I avoid any drink with sugar and just keep it simple with milk and water. I don't take any supplements except for a multivitamin with my lunch. That's it. That's my entire diet. It may seem incredibly bland, but that's the point. I purposely chose a plain and boring diet to follow so that my brain doesn't get excited to eat food, so eating is just a time to get nutrients inside of my body instead of a time to spend money on things that taste good. This also leaves more space and dopamine in my brain to pursue other things that I want to do that give me dopamine, including writing this book.

Go Running

Besides the obvious benefits of just being a generally healthy person, running will also make you more spiritual. Just live in the moment when you're doing it. Feel what your body is feeling, feel the good endorphins, the pain, and everything else. It's a primitive thing to do, because in the modern world we don't really have any scary predators to run away from. It makes you feel human. It has anti-depressive capabilities and I can tell you for a fact that when you're keeping up with your fitness and health, it's entirely easier to connect with your higher self. You're sending signals, even if they are subconscious, that you love yourself. Why would you want to run and eat healthy if you don't care about yourself?

Sports like running offer you a great opportunity for full-body awareness. Your mind and your body can get entirely immersed in the present moment. Challenge yourself to stay with the experience. Experience the sensations without calling them 'pain'. When you're mindful of the present moment, the distinctions between mind and body begin to disappear and yield to an awareness of being.

Spend Time with Nature

Us humans are not the only things that were put on Earth. Because we spend most of our time looking into phone screens, Televisions, and Computers, we tend to forget that there's a whole world out there. Spending time with nature is a great way to get to know yourself and other forms of creation. I spent most of my childhood in the city and if you're like me, then just seeing buildings all the time are the norm. They are perfect, symmetrical creations of humankind. They aren't natural. Observe the things in nature and then compare them to human inventions. In the military, we learned to camouflage our helmets and weapons with leaves and other foliage to make them look more natural, because a gun is a very carefully crafting, near perfect invention that cannot be possible in nature. So we camouflaged them to blend into nature and avoid detection by the enemy. Observe what nature is like. Sometimes it's perfect. Sometimes it's not. Most likely you are able to see it and observe it in all of its beauty. If you can't see it, then you can smell it, touch it, and hear it. If you are struggling to find beauty and good in your life, then I would strongly suggest spending as much time in nature and with other people, preferably both, and as little time with electronics as possible. If you live deep in a city, even as much as driving to a park on a weekend is better than nothing at all.

See Things for What They Are

Try not to glamorize things. Philosophers in the 19th century called this idealism, and it runs rampant today. It means that the way you think of something, or someone, is far more 'glamorous' or valuable than it is in reality. The bad does not come from your high expectations, but rather from getting let down from those expectations. If you buy a sports car that will never get you over 23 miles per gallon, then you're not going to get mad at the car for costing you so much money in gas. That's because you knew that was one of the downsides of buying the car. That's just what the car is, it's fast but it costs you money to maintain.

PART IV: MEDITATE

There are more than one ways to meditate. You can meditate while you're walking and you can meditate while doing anything you want. But I'm going to give you a basic guide on meditating with the primary focus of achieving a higher state of consciousness and connecting with your inner self. Understand that this is a practice, and you have to work at it to achieve optimal results and growth. It's like playing a guitar, it just doesn't take as long. When you first start out you'll figure things out and learn new things about yourself and the world, but it will take time for you to rise in your level of consciousness and reach a higher state of being. Understand that nothing in life that is worthy of achieving is free or easy or both. Things take time to heal and grow just like your brain when recovering from a drug addiction or a severed relationship with a once close friend. You have to want to grow, however. Like a tree sprouting from a small sapling and transforming over time to become a blossoming home of birds and bees, an integral part of nature that is one with all of creation.

You can start by getting a chair and placing it in front of a wall. A wall works but you could also set it down facing anything you want, could be nature, could be the television. Just make sure that your electronics are off and there are no external distractions that could disturb you. You could also sit on the ground cross legged if you like but I prefer the chair. Sit down in your chosen position, make sure your posture is good, sit upright. Lift your shoulders up and then roll them back. Place your hands on your lap or just simply palms down on your thigh. Keep your eyes open to start and just sit there and exist. Focus on your breath, and make sure that you're breathing properly through your nose. You want to just sit there and exist. A good rule is that if your eyes are moving, you're doing too much. Just sit there with your eyes focused on one thing but thinking of nothing. Thoughts about the past and future will find their way into their mind, but pay them no attention. You are now existing in the present moment. You may think about feelings that you felt recently or your thoughts about others in your life may find themselves in your thoughts as well. Do not judge these thoughts, instead just think of them as neither good nor bad, just let them be. This way you can observe yourself from a non-judgemental angle because you're not judging your own thoughts that are unfairly influenced by how you're feeling and how external factors are influencing your life. You may come to a realization about your life even after your first session of meditation.

One of my first realizations was that you don't need anything to be happy. I was just happy as I was, sitting there meditating. I didn't have a college education yet and I didn't have as much knowledge and life experiences as I do now but I realized that happiness is not something that you can achieve eternally but simply a feeling that comes and goes, like any other feeling. Life is meant to be enjoyed and embraced, no matter how you're feeling. Life is supposed to have struggle and hardship and discomfort sometimes, because that's what makes us human. If you were happy all the time, every hour of every day, that would just become your new normal and the emotion of happiness or excitement would disappear. You would have nothing to be excited about. Embrace the ideas and outlooks on life that come to you during meditation because in this state, you're experiencing your true self, unhindered by your current emotions and connected to your inner being.

PART V: GRATITUDE

What's there to be Grateful For?

Have gratitude for every moment. You don't have to be alive right now. There's nothing in the universe existing that says that you have to be alive right now, so embrace life. After all, it could be taken away from you at any moment.

A big part of gratitude is just not wanting things. In Buddhism the 'Three Fires' are greed, hatred, and delusion. I think that hatred and delusion are more human concepts, but greed is the one that leads to most of the world's evil. Don't look at what your neighbour has and become resentful, use it as motivation to improve your own life. Don't take for granted all of the blessings that you have.

I like to be grateful for just simply having food in my stomach, clothes that provide warmth, a house to stay in, and not being cold and wet all the time. I have two arms, and two feet and they all work. These limbs give me the ability to work, create, live, and love. For me, that is enough. Oftentimes we feel dissatisfied with our current situations because we don't have a particular material possession, or maybe it's someone that we love that doesn't love us back. We forget about all the things that we do have, and how lucky we are to be born in this day and age. It's a fact life now is more comfortable than it has ever been for our ancestors. We have air conditioning, central air, a huge food supply, and all of the world's knowledge at our fingertips. The world is hugely accessible, save for a few countries and you can communicate with another human instantly thousands of miles away via phone or video call. In other words, it's a great time to be a human.

There's evidence that shows that having less desires in your life will produce far more happiness and wellbeing than having a lot of material possessions. That's why you can visit a remote tribe that has been for the most part in isolation and see that they are oftentimes more happy than people that live in big cities and have access to all the comforts of the first world. The difference is that these remote tribes don't have as many wants and desires that give them that feeling of dissatisfaction or discomfort in their lives. You can be like that too, just make up your mind that you don't want to have that thing that you want so badly but you can't afford to buy yet. For now, all I want is to be a good man and be able to provide for my family. That's it, there's nothing else in the world that I honestly can say that I want right now. Sure, there are things that I would like to have, but I don't need them. There's plenty of time for me to get money and go on vacation in Fiji or Hawaii. This world has a lot of money in it and you have lots of time to make money, but what you don't have is replenishable time to make up for the years that you spent being unhappy or believing that you weren't handed a good enough deck in life.

Cutting Things Out

Believe it or not, one of the fastest ways to achieve better well-being in your life is to get rid of things. I already talked about getting rid of negative people and influences, but now I want to talk about things. We live in a very materialist society, very heavily focused on the things that we have. It's how you get popular and achieve social acceptance easily. However, as you may have already realized, having things and getting new things only leads to you wanting more things. This ties back into your dopamine binary system of wanting stuff. Your brain gets a sort of 'high' from getting a thing and the social acceptance that the thing provides and then your brain doesn't keep continuing to generate dopamine once you've gotten that thing. Your brain didn't make the dopamine because you have the thing, it only got the dopamine feel good chemicals because you got it and you were excited about getting it. You need to rewire your brain to stop this cycle of always wanting things. We always want more stuff and better stuff because there's always going to be more and better stuff available to provide that dopamine to you.

Look at actual wealthy people, for example. I'm not talking about well-off people that perhaps own a business and make upwards of 100k a year. I'm talking about actual wealthy people that sign the rich people's paychecks. You'll notice that they don't really look wealthy or act like it either. Most of them drive modest cars and live comfortably but they don't try to keep up with the Joneses. That's because they've surpassed that level of trying to validate yourself by getting a lot of stuff.

PART VI: MINDFULNESS

Live in the Moment

Try not to think about what's going to happen or what you need to do later. I like to think in terms of the next hour but a good rule of thumb when first practicing mindfulness is to think in terms of five minutes. Just worry about what you have to do within the next five minutes. Immerse yourself in the task at hand. It doesn't have to make you feel good, just accept it for what it is no matter how hard it is. If you don't believe in a religion I want you to go through the next five minutes and focus entirely on what you're doing. If you are Christian, go through the next five minutes doing whatever you're doing and only thinking of God if you need to think about anything not relating to the moment.

Thinking of the past will make you depressed and thinking of the future will make you anxious. Understand that you are a human and you cannot go back in time. You cannot speed time up and make the future come faster. Thus, these are two things that you cannot control so the best thing to do is to not worry about it. Only worry about the things you can control. Really think about that. Think about the things you grieve over that you have zero control over. What's the point in grieving? Yes, the outcome might be unfavorable, but you can't change it. There's no good or bad, only what is. We might think of a situation to be good or bad based on the illusion of emotion, but understand that these are earthly processes and remind yourself to not let your inner constitution be affected or put off course by these simple thoughts.

Marcus Aurelias, the famous Roman Emperor that wrote the book *"Meditations"*, often liked to compare his life to the existence of the entire universe. He often contemplated death in his works and often reminded himself of how little time he really has. He says that if his life lasts sixty years, then just imagine how short that is in comparison to all of existence. He's right. There has been an infinite amount of time that has elapsed before your birth, and so too will there be infinite time after your death. Your entire lifespan is just a little invisible dot on that timeline. Live every day to the fullest because you don't know when you're going to die. Not that you should fear death, but appreciate the gift of life because you don't necessarily have to be alive. The world will continue to go forth after your death just as it has gone for eons before your birth. All of that money that you're worried about making will not follow you into your death, it will stay right here on Earth in this universe, and so it is not eternal and everlasting and thus it is not true.

Meditation and time spent in nature are great ways to live in the moment. You can live in the moment and be mindful in doing anything, however. It's as simple as focusing on your task and not being somewhere else. Be present, here, on Earth. By doing this you'll be eliminating a large portion of suffering that's caused by 'desire' or 'want' for things that we can't have, such as re-doing things that happened in the past or not having enough money to buy that super cool thing that you want to buy.

I have clothes on my back, food in my stomach, and two arms and two feet. I'm writing this book, and I'm in heaven because that's all that I could possibly need. The world is breaking down around me, the Corona Virus is spreading like a fire in every nation, and people are exuding negativity all around me. They are worried, anxious because they lost their jobs or fear the illness. My grandparents send me pictures and videos of hospitals in Italy full of people and mass burial sites. They are openly accepting grief caused by something that is not in their power to control.

Balance

Understand that everything in life is based on balance. What comes up has got to come down. If you do wrong to others, don't be surprised if that wrongdoing comes back around to bite you. If you do good things to lift others up instead of bringing them down, that will come back around to you too. Whether you believe in karma or not, this ideal of 'what goes around comes around' is always true. Look at it this way, if you help others and practice respect and kindness all the time, there's a much, much higher chance that others will return that same attitude to you.

You can apply this principle to more than just spirituality and the idea of 'good' karma or 'bad' karma. If you sit down and don't exercise for a long time, your body will no doubt fall out of balance and become lazy and uncomfortable all the time. If you work out too much, your body is going to ache and you'll be punished for that too later down the road when your joints start to give out.

My favorite rugby player in the world is somewhat of a legend at my college. He played in the 1970s and played a huge role in the development of our program's history. He passed away recently, but I will never forget the positivity that he brought to our program. Back when he played rugby, he was big and strong. The last time I saw him before he passed away, he was elderly and in a wheelchair. This is just a part of nature, and it made me sad to talk to him because I realized that someday, that's going to be me. Someday, that's going to be my kids. Us humans are obsessed with immortality, which is mostly a western idea. We are obsessed with having a permanent place on Earth. In Tibet, a common practice is to let vultures devour the dead, and to let young children watch this process and meditate on it to demonstrate that nothing lasts forever. Many Asian societies firmly understand the importance of teaching impermanence.

Life is all about balance and change, both of these things. It's only according to nature, and nothing that is according to nature is evil.

Benefits of being Mindful:

- You can pay attention to the reality of the present moment with peace and clarity.
- You go away from narration mode and towards experience mode. That is, you redirect your attention from the

past and future and towards the richness of the present moment.
- You become less reactive to your environment and more relaxed.
- You become more self-attuned, and become able to direct your attention to areas of your life that are lacking.
- You enter a state of security, ready to accept whatever life throws your way.

PART VII: YOU WILL NOT BE HAPPY

Yes, you read that correctly. A better way to put it is that you will not be happy all the time. You need to understand that happiness is seen as something that is attainable, as if you can reach a certain point in your life and just be happy until you die. This is far from the truth and it's a pill that you need to swallow if you want eternal peace in your life.

Happiness is just an emotion, just like all the other emotions. It's no different from anger, sadness, and grief, only dictated by outside factors in your life. If you have a lot of money, that money will not make you happy. If you have a lot of fame and popularity, that won't make you happy either. It's a feeling that comes and goes just like the rest. Instead, focus on being grateful all the time and content with what you have. Let happiness come and go and enjoy it while it lasts. It's part of being human. It's meant so that you can savour the important moments and transitions that you are experiencing in your life, whether that be getting married, getting a new job you really like, or achieving something that you worked hard for. You can't be happy all the time, and you shouldn't want to be. If you were happy all the time you'd be like a robot, just feeling the same way all day every day. You would forget what it's like to be human and that immense joy would become your new normal.

Don't try to chase happiness. Instead, focus your attention on doing what you really want to do with your life. If you aren't sure of what you want to do, make the decision to put away all of your electronics for a day, maybe on a Sunday when you have no homework or work obligations, and meditate and spend some quality time with yourself and nature. At the end of the day, make some phone calls to people that really matter to you. Do what brings you fulfillment and meaning in your life because meaning and fulfillment are not congruent with happiness. Say you want to have kids and be a rockstar, spend your free time focusing on everything that will enable you to do this stuff. A goal like that isn't easy. You're going to have to save a lot of money, maybe start your own business so that you can sustain yourself while you're putting all that time and money into your band and recording equipment. Once, you're set up well enough, you have your kids and your band and you're writing some music, then that's all you'll need to be happy because that's what you decided that you want to do with your life. This is just one example. One of the best things about living in the 21st century is that you can be literally anything that you want to, it's just a matter of how much you're willing to commit to it.

I remember a conversation with a close friend I had while working as an armorer in the military. We often had deep conversations in that hot, secluded box where the rifles were kept. He thought that it was insane that I wouldn't trade my life for anyone else's. "No, I wouldn't trade spots with Brad Pitt", I told him. He thought I was lying but I was serious as Brad himself in

Fight Club. My friend was convinced that wealth is what brought happiness, and that's why he wasn't happy in that moment.

I understood that happiness is just an emotion that comes and goes and to chase fulfillment instead, which is why I am absolutely okay in my own skin and I love to live my own life. It's like a story that I'm writing as I go, with my own experiences shaping it. Why would I want to live in someone else's story?

Happiness is found in Doing things not possessing them.

Dukkha

Dukkha is a Buddhist concept and it is most often translated as 'suffering'. It can mean suffering in terms of bad health, sickness, and poverty. However, it more importantly goes beyond those more obvious forms of suffering. It can also mean the perpetual and seemingly eternal dissatisfaction that is present in every moment of your life. The Buddha described Dukkha as a feeling that you get from the very meaning of the actual word. 'Du' means bad and 'Ka' means wheel. The Buddha connects a metaphor of having a bad wheel on a cart to how you feel every day. Imagine you're riding on a horse or ox drawn cart and there is one bad wheel, negatively influencing every movement of the cart. Maybe it's damaged, missing a piece, or a little bit off of it's axle. Your cart is going to be bumpy and you're going to be uncomfortable the whole entire ride. To the Buddhists, this kind of dissatisfaction that we feel in life is self-inflicted and comes from a misunderstanding of what life is all about. We don't understand how nature works so we always feel like something is missing in a way, or our life is lacking something. It's like a background feeling that is present in every experience.

This kind of feeling means that much of our happiness and comfort in life is contingent on outside factors, things we can't control. The good news is that this sense can be corrected! Don't worry about things you can't control and don't be happy just because people like you. If you're happy because people like you then your happiness is dependent on them liking you, thus you will always feel like you need to keep their approval or make them happy all the time or you'll lose your own happiness.

Happiness is one of those things that we usually want to cling on to. I would argue strongly against clinging onto anything at all. In referral to happiness, sadness, and other emotions, Marcus Aurelias said that you should observe the sensations, and not resist them, for they are only natural. However, he urges us to not let the 'ruling part' (your brain) add to the sensation that it is either good or bad.

Self Acceptance

Take a look again at nature. Nothing in nature is perfect. There is no perfection to be found on Earth. Modern generations are plagued with self hate caused by things like social media that force us to compare ourselves to other people. We are exposed to people who we perceive as better than us, maybe they have more followers or a nicer home and car, or maybe they just have the friendship and family that we don't. We always try to strive toward perfection and fail to realise that it's good to love ourselves.

We forget the gifts that we do have, and often don't appreciate what we can give to the world.

What I Learned From Other Cultures

Nothing can be lost by trying to understand other cultures than your own. Doing so will bring you closer to the way that they understand the world and it will only enlighten you. It's easy and it's comfortable to only be friends and have connections with people that are from the same place as you, look like you, and talk like you. I say you should go out of that comfort zone and try to talk to people that are from somewhere else. It's likely that they'll think of things way different than you do and by asking them about their culture you'll come to understand why they think the way that they do.

I have about a dozen friends from Saudi Arabia. They are cadets like me, but the difference is they serve their own country and I serve mine. They explained to me that many people from Arabia think that Americans are greedy. They shared that in their culture, when you're offered something like a gift or a favor, you're not supposed to accept immediately. That's seen as rude and greedy. Instead, you deny them 3-4 times before finally accepting. Just knowing this sparked some light bulbs in my brain and I can now understand why they always deny me when I offer them help. I just have to ask them 4 more times and then they'll accept. This custom is to ensure that when you offer to help someone, it is genuine because you're not going to offer a gift four times that you're not sure about giving someone. This also means that relationships in their culture are oftentimes more 'invested' than what we have in the West. People remember the good favors that you give them and are more likely to return it and keep the friendship strong.

Chinese history is vastly different from American and European history. Throughout Chinese history, the country oftentimes experienced periods of hardship followed by periods of prosperity, then back to hardship. This up-down kind of past has become a part of their traditional knowledge of how the world works and as a result, Chinese people are more comfortable in times of hardship than we are. They understand that things aren't always good and they aren't always bad. They can survive and thrive in hardship better than we can, because we're not used to it. Throughout American history, going all the way back to the colonies, we've enjoyed an unprecedented standard for individual wealth that is hard to compare to any other country at any other point in time. We've also enjoyed global dominance as a world power for about one hundred years straight now. China has been more up-down, sometimes being the most dominant influencer and competitor in the world as they knew it, and at other times being subject to foreign invasions, conquests, and tyrannical rulers. As Americans, I think it's safe to say that whenever we endure serious hardship, we tend to easily get depressed and think that it's the end of the world. We don't have a good understanding of the way the world works and how there is always a balance. What comes up always has to come down. There is no good or bad, only what exists.

What Should I do if I'm Depressed?

The answer I'm going to give you is going to be unconventional and it may even hurt a little. The good news is every time I've given this advice to someone, it worked, including myself. You're not going to get it from a doctor or psychiatrist. They want your money so they won't tell you this.

You're depressed because you're most likely experiencing one of these three things. Either 1) You're not connected to your higher self because of some sort of addiction, 2) Your body isn't getting enough food, water, sunlight, exercise, and social interaction for proper wellbeing, or 3) You can't seem to find purpose in your life. Note that all three of these problems are greatly exacerbated by the availability of easy dopamine such as junk food, video games, your phone, the internet, drugs like weed and alcohol, and the biggest one, social media. They make your problems worse because they provide you with a temporary dopamine hit and trick your brain into thinking it's doing amazing at life. What do I mean by this? It's simple. The high calorie and sugar junk food makes your brain think it's consuming a high calorie meal, so it sends a 'yes' signal to your brain, telling it to do more of that. The likes and engagement you get on social media tell your brain that you're getting acceptance from the tribe, and hence your odds of survival are greatly increased. The video games give you an artificial way of 'leveling up', or so to say, progress in life and go on adventures, which is a critical part of the human experience.

This book isn't about depression, it's about spirituality, but the good thing is that spirituality is going to ward off depression greater than any prescription drug can. When you experience the feeling of waking up when you're connected to your higher self, you'll experience an orgasmic pulse throughout your entire body. You'll want to get up and go do stuff and accomplish things. Things like drugs and pointless showboating on social media become repulsive to you.

PART VIII: CHANGE

The sun comes up every day and then it has to go down. The leaves on the trees bloom in Spring and then they wither away in Winter. My apartment is by a lake, I've seen generations of ducks come into the world and then depart it. Change is all around us, and yet we are still afraid of it. We don't like to accept change as a normal part of life on Earth.

With time comes change. Both are inevitable. We are weary of the uncertain and prefer to accept what we already know. Scientifically, the reason for this is because the brain is more comfortable doing what it already knows and going places it's already been. This is the wrong way to look at life. Look around at nature. It's always changing. Observe the animals and the trees and the weather. The animals are born and then they die. The trees and flowers grow and one day wither. The weather changes constantly to facilitate the will of the universe. You too will one day die, so understand that you do not have an infinite amount of time. Why should a human have apprehension about change? Change is according to nature, and nothing is evil which is according to nature.

Energies

Maybe up until now you haven't paid much attention to the energies that people and emotions bring into your life. Maybe you have and want to understand it more. The more in tune you are with your higher self, and the less plugged in you are to the illusion of the world and your ego, the better you are at judging energies. It can be the energy in a room, or the energy of a coworker or friend. It gets easier and easier to identify negative energies that you wouldn't want around you, and just cut them off or ignore them entirely.

Dealing with Negative Energy

As you reach a higher vibration, you can sense the vibration of others, too. It becomes easy and second nature to tell when another person is experiencing a very low state of vibration or energy. The further you go on your spiritual journey is the easier this ability becomes for you. You can then choose to get rid of negative energies and avoid negative spaces that don't add value to your life. You may now clearly see the kind of negative energy that someone is bringing into your life that you couldn't see before. You may have thought in the past that "That's just how they are", or "They must mean something else" when they try to put you down. Since you're more spiritually connected with your higher self and realize that you don't need people like that in your life, you can easily disconnect from them. I always pray for people while I'm disconnecting from them. I always pray before going to bed and I'll pray that they are protected on their journeys in life, and wish them the best. Marcus Aurelias said in *Meditations* that "The best way to avenge thyself is to not become like the wrongdoer". He means that wishing them the best and not returning their negativity is the best way to exact revenge upon yourself for the wrong they have done you. Not letting them affect you and exuding positivity into their negativity is, to me, one of the highest possible virtues that you can act on.

People are Going to Hate You

People always hate winners. People are going to call you full of yourself or arrogant. They're always going to try to put you down because you aren't afraid to stand up for yourself and what you know is right. When you're shining bright, you might not realize it but to other people, you're making them look dull.

Think about the Patriots and Tom Brady. Think of how many people hate Tom Brady. You know who doesn't hate Tom Brady? Patriots fans. He's a winner, he makes other teams look bad. What's important is to never dumb yourself down or underperform to purposely make others feel better. Instead, since you have positive energy, spread that energy to them. It may take some time but you'll see that this kind of energy and attitude is going to come back around to you. Remember that if you're winning and what you've accomplished is true, then it's not cocky or arrogant because it's true. Don't be afraid to put the pressure on yourself to say that you're going to accomplish something you know you can accomplish. Hold yourself accountable and follow through.

They won't like you more and you definitely won't like yourself more by cheating yourself out of an accomplishment. When other people who aren't happy see you enjoying your life, they won't know why you're happy and content with life but they'll want to put you down to their level. Understand this, and understand that the best response is to ignore it and then always wish them the best. Maybe even call to check up on them. Whatever you do, just don't go down to their level and entertain them because that's exactly what they wanted. Once you do that, you've proved to them that you're no better than they are.

Sex Transmutation

This chapter is mainly directed towards young men, but I believe that every single human can learn a thing or two about sex transmutation.

Chapter 11 of Napoleon Hill's famous book 'Think and Grow Rich' talks about the mystery of sexual energy toward getting rich and accomplishing things. I think there's much more to it than just a mystery and you can transmute your energy toward much more than simply work or business.

The 21st century is hyper-sexualized. Everywhere you look, you see sex or images related to sex. You see sexual innuendos on billboards and people dressed in provocative clothing in ads online. Why is this? The answer is simple. Sex sells. It gets your attention and it gets clicks. By bringing the emotion of sex into your mind, it excites your natural instinct to reproduce for the continuation of the species and to act as a therapeutic relaxant, and rightfully so because sex with a partner is the most therapeutic and sedating thing that can be achieved naturally.

You can harness your sexual energy and redirect that energy and attention to other areas of your life that are lacking, or simply to any kind of creative outlet or endeavour. You don't have to stop thinking about sex, just redirect that lust and desire into other areas of your life. As Napoleon Hill says in his book about getting rich, the desire for sex is "A river that may be dammed, and its water controlled for a time but eventually, it will force an outlet.".

It's easier than it sounds. I'm going to be blunt here when I say that porn or any other outlet for your fantasies are literally one click away. It's a good thing you've developed discipline from putting down your phone and hopping in the cold shower, because this one takes discipline. Refrain from acts that drain you of your sexual energy and watch yourself naturally connect more to your higher self.

When I quit porn and masturbation when I was sixteen, I suddenly had the energy to do the things I really wanted to do, like reading my bible and putting more effort into wrestling and working out. I wasn't lazy anymore. It's like an improvement pill or secret that people will try to sell you but it's free. If you're married or in a relationship, you might find yourself becoming more intimate and connected with your partner.

If you can successfully refrain from engaging in cheap and meaningless outlets for sex energy, including porn, you will attain a skill that most people in this generation all the ones after it will likely never master. That's because it's never taught in schools. The porn industry is only getting richer, and has billions to invest in campaigns to publish articles and studies claiming that masturabtion is good and healthy, and that it decreases your risk for prostate cancer and increases wellbeing. It's like the cigarettes of the 21st century, turning us into addicted zombies that depend on pixels on a screen for enjoyment rather than simply existing on a higher plane of existence and enjoying life for what it is. Think about that for a minute. They will do anything to keep you addicted to porn. Why do you think it's free? The hook is always easily accessible, these industries are not stupid.

I know that this last paragraph isn't an easy to swallow pill, because you're just now considering the possibility that you've been lied to your entire life, but that's okay. It's going to hurt. Let it hurt. That's how you grow.

PART IX: LIVE YOUR LIFE

Life is too short for you to grieve over a small loss or become anxious of a specific outcome. Do everything you do with purpose and fire and fury. Experience all emotions in their purity. Yes, be angry, be excited, and be sad. It's going to hurt. Let it hurt. Be aware and present in the moment, that's how you live. Worrying about the past and future and things you cannot change is not living, that's only existing.

Before you know it you'll be forty, and you're going to feel what it's like to not be full of energy all the time. Not long after that you'll be sixty and then seventy. You're going to be glad you did things that constituted actual life. You'll be sour if you don't and you'll regret not taking that cross country trip with your friends or maybe not making that Youtube channel you always wanted to make.

Contemplate

So by now you know what you need to do. You should have a solid idea of the changes that you need to make to your life to get the results that you want in regards to how spiritual connectedness and discovering your higher self. I can't wait for you to meet your higher self, I can bet that you're going to fall in love with them and never go back.

You're not anxious and you're not depressed because that's just how you are. No human is born that way. You were conditioned to be that way because of our environment. No one's to blame for that, so don't feel angry or resentful for it. You just need to recognize that the problem is you and that you need to take control. Yes, I said it. You should blame yourself for your problems because that's the only way you can move forward. You can forgive yourself and move on, sculpting yourself into the man or woman that you want to be. Nobody dreams his or her self into a well-rounded human being, they sculpt themselves into one and it's going to hurt. Be mad at other people or society and see how far that's going to get you. Just observe it and quietly do what you know that you need to do. You can let others continue to engage in self-deprecating behavior and put themselves into debt to make fancy Instagram content. Let them pretend to be someone they're not, and let them go through their lives seeking physical, simplistic pleasures like drugs and sex to because that's what they think makes them happy.

It shouldn't take you getting to rock bottom like I did to discover spirituality. It doesn't have to and it should never have to. You just have to decide for yourself that it's something you're ready for. When I was at home alone, depressed, uncertain whether I'd get my high school diploma or not, going through my parent's divorce, the words inside of my Bible were the one thing that kept me going. I'll never forget the radiency of the words and how they all came together to make sense. I realized that what happened to me was the best thing that ever happened in my life. I was doing the wrong thing and making mistakes, and I was saved by the consequence. It hurt to get through and recover from, but without it I don't know where I would be right now. More than likely I wouldn't be in college; I definitely wouldn't be in the Army. I took what I learned about respect and love for others from the Bible and implemented it in my life. I now enjoy a healthy relationship with everyone in my family who's close to me and supports me. These are things I didn't know how to do. I, like most kids, wasn't raised by my mother and my father. I was raised by the internet, my peers at school, and video games, I just lived with my mother and father.

TO CONCLUDE

I hope that you learned how to be more connected to your higher self. I hope that the world makes a little more sense to you now. Many people may read this book, only a few may read it. I don't care. If I only helped one, singular person make a change to better their lives, then my mission is accomplished.

So go out into the world, expose yourself to things you've never been exposed to, take risks. Don't have a risk-averse mindset. Don't sell yourself short by sticking to what you already know and sticking with old habits. When you love yourself and respect yourself, it's easy to do these things. You don't care what people think, you're not what they say you are.

Ask yourself what it is you truly want, and take that first step to make it a reality.

"You can't live in paradise- but you are living right here. Make this your paradise or make this your hell. The choice is entirely yours. Really."

ACKNOWLEDGEMENTS

This book is dedicated to Kaheel, one of my best friends growing up. We were nine years old when you died, when you left your physical body. You died early, and there is so much that you didn't get to do, so much life that you didn't get to experience. I still miss you man. You wanted to be a car racing driver, an ultimate rockstar. I know that you're there, even if not physically. I know that you're proud of me for doing what I always wanted to do, too.

I'd like to thank my parents for always encouraging me with whatever I set my mind to do. I don't always have the best ideas, but I appreciate the support throughout the years for all of my endeavors. I am thankful every day that you are both alive and healthy, and that your voice is only a phone call away.

Thanks Michelle, you're like a third parent to me. You taught me temperance, responsibility, and the importance of self-love and care. We don't always see eye to eye but that's okay. You were always there for me when I needed you, and I owe you eternally.

Finally, thanks Isaias. It's hard to come across good quality amigos like you. We always push each other forward and bring each other up instead of dragging each other down. It's amazing how we feed off of one another's energy and success. Driving across the country with you in the middle of a global pandemic was awesome. I think our greatest achievement so far was turning Jake into a certified killer in less than a year.

Made in United States
Troutdale, OR
12/07/2023